Content

1

3

Acknowledgments

I am truly blessed to have a wonderful family and friends in my life to remind me that I am never alone. First and foremost, I wish to acknowledge, with sincere appreciation, my husband Robert. You demonstrated the patience of a saint while I worked on this project. Much love and gratitude to my son and daughter, Kenneth and Debra, for encouraging me to follow my dreams. A big thank you to my sisters and brothers, Marie, George, Betty, Johnny, Rebecca and willie, for being my taste-testers when I created unusual and different foods. You always did it with a smile. For my granddaughter Natilie for inspiration and support and for Kenneth Shurrod for devouring the fruits of my labor. And for Lyndal; gone but not forgotten.

Introduction

The ranks of people who abstain from all animal products are rapidly growing. Scientific research shows that health benefits drastically increase as the amount of food from animal sources in the diet decreases; making vegan diets among the healthiest in the world.

After a lifelong struggle with an eating disorder, I went from yo-yo dieting to eating a diet consisting of mostly processed foods. I knew I needed to change my relationship with food for the better. But at the same time, all I could think was this is how someone my age was supposed to feel. Someone once said to me, "Look at your mother. That is how you are going to look at that age." And so I believed that the weight was in my genes. It was just to be expected that I would have aching joints from arthritis and be tired most of the time. I would have to accept that I'd have to see my doctor at least once a month and endure high cholesterol and blood pressure. I simply didn't know how to change.

Then, one day while at a friend's home, my friend put on a video of "*An Introduction to Hallelujah Acres: Teaching Health from a Biblical Perspective.*" After watching the film, I immediately took control of my health and began paying attention to my body's nutritional needs. I replaced the foods I had been told all of my life were good for me. To start, I replaced dairy milk with non-dairy alternatives like almond and coconut milk. I replaced white sugar with agave and pure maple syrup. Enriched white flour was replaced with whole wheat flour and whole grain oat flour.

When I made the choice to change my eating habits to a whole food vegan lifestyle, the transformation in myself was unbelievable. After eating a plant-based diet for only three weeks, my arthritic joints didn't ache anymore. My energy level soared to new heights. My skin started to glow, and I felt better than I had felt in a long time. I could walk for two miles without having to stop and rest. This was brand new for me. I was feeling so good that I wanted to tell my family, friends and some of my church members. I wanted them to know they didn't have to be sick and tired all of the time. So I began studying to become a Certified Health Minister through Hallelujah Acres.

After getting my Certification from Hallelujah Acres, my co-workers and I organized a plant-based potluck lunch at

8

my place of employment. Every Monday, we fixed a vegan lunch or purchased something from Whole Foods. My co-workers sometimes met me in the hallway and asked me when I was going to bring more of "the food I eat." The Activities Director approached me one day and said, "I had some of your food, when is your book coming out?"

I had never thought of writing a cookbook, but at that moment, the seed was planted, and here it is. Thanks, Earl!

Part One

Understanding Veganism

What is a Vegan?

A vegan is someone who doesn't eat, use, wear or otherwise consume anything of animal origin. Vegans avoid all products resulting from animal exploitation. Examples of things that vegans avoid are meat, dairy, eggs, oil, gelatin, etc. It's more of a lifestyle than a diet. Vegans also avoid buying products that come from animals, avoiding clothing with, silk, wool, leather, or fur. Vegans will typically opt for personal care products and household cleaners that are not tested on animals. Vegans do eat lots of fruits, vegetables, grains, beans, seeds, and nuts. Some Vegans will also avoid certain vaccines; the production of the flu vaccine, for example, involves the use of hen eggs. Depending on their circumstances, vegans may donate non-vegan items to charities, or use them until they wear out.

The Ethics of Veganism

Ethical vegans state that the production of eggs and dairy causes animal suffering and premature death. In both *battery cage* and *free-range egg* production, most male *chicks are killed,* because they will not lay eggs, and there is no financial incentive for a producer to keep them.
To obtain milk from *dairy cattle*, cows are kept pregnant through *artificial insemination* to prolong lactation. Male calves are slaughtered at birth, separated from their mother for veal production, or reared for beef. Female calves are separated from their mothers within 24-48

hours of birth and fed milk replacement so that the cow's milk is retained for human consumption. After five years or so, they are slaughtered, to be made into ground meat products. Without being used in these ways, they might otherwise live for 20 years or more.

The Vegan Diet

Vegan diets tend to be higher in Dietary Fiber, Magnesium, Folic Acid, Vitamin C, Vitamin E, Iron, and Photochemical, and lower in calories, saturated fat, cholesterol, long-chain omega-3 fatty acids, Vitamin D, Calcium, Zinc, and Vitamin B-12. A well-planned vegan diet can reduce the risk of heart disease and is regarded as appropriate for all stages of the life cycle by the American

Dietetic Association, the Australian National Health and Medical Research Council, and Dietitians of Canada. Because uncontaminated plant foods do not provide Vitamin B-12 (which is produced by microorganisms such as bacteria), researchers agree that vegans should eat B-12 fortified foods or take a daily B-12 supplement.

Iron

Vegan diets generally contain more iron than Vegetarian diets because dairy products (avoided in a vegan diet) contain very little iron. According to the Vegetarian Resource Group, high-iron foods suitable for vegans include black strap molasses, lentils, tofu, quinoa, kidney beans, and chickpeas. Nutritionist Tom Sanders writes that iron absorption can be enhanced by eating a source of vitamin-C along with a plant source of

14

iron, and by avoiding eating anything that would inhibit iron absorption. Sources of vitamin-C include half a cup of cauliflower or five fluid ounces of orange juice. Plant sources of iron include soybeans, tofu, tempeh and black beans. Some herbal teas and coffee can inhibit iron absorption, as can spices that contain tannins, turmeric, coriander, chilies, and marine.

Calcium

Calcium is needed to maintain bone health and for a number of metabolic functions including muscle function, vascular contractions, vasodilation, nerve transmission, intra-cellular signaling and hormone secretion. Ninety-nine percent of the body's calcium is stored in the bones and teeth. Vegans are advised to eat three servings per day of a high-calcium food such as fortified, organic almond milk, organic tofu, raw almonds or hazelnuts. It is also advised to take supplements as needed. Plant sources include broccoli, turnips, cabbage, and kale. Contrary to popular belief, the bio-availability of calcium in spinach is poor. Whole wheat bread is also a source of calcium, though it does not provide large amounts of the nutrient.

Vitamin D

Vitamin D is needed for several functions. One of the biggest tasks for Vitamin D is to aid in calcium absorption. It is also responsible for enabling mineralization of bones, and bone growth. Without it, bones can become thin and brittle. Together with calcium, it offers protection against osteoporosis. Vitamin D is produced in the body when ultraviolet rays from the sun hit the skin; outdoor exposure is needed because UVB radiation does not penetrate glass. Most vegan diets contain little or no vitamin D, unless the food is fortified, so supplements maybe needed depending on exposure to sunlight.

Vitamin B-12

Vitamin B-12 is a bacterial product needed for cell division, the formation and maturation of red blood cells, the synthesis of DNA, and normal nerve function. A deficiency can lead to several health problems including megaloblastic anemia and nerve damage. The consensus among nutritionists is that vegans should eat food *fortified with B-12 or use a supplement.*

Where do Vegans get their Protein?

The question vegans get asked the most is "Where do you get your protein?" We can get as much as we need from the foods we eat, like *beans, nuts, seeds, grains, soy and even greens.* Many people think or have been told we need *exorbitant* amounts of protein: way more than is recommended by the FDA. But if you look at the recommendation, they're not that high at all. The US Recommended Daily Allowance of protein is 0.36 grams per pound of body weight. Tempeh is much higher in protein than tofu, seitan, and legumes. Below is a list of some vegan sources of protein.

Vegan Foods for Protein (from the *Vegetarian Resource Group*)

Lentils- 18 grams/cup
Chickpeas- 12 grams/cup
Tempeh- 41 grams/cup
Black beans- 15 grams/cup
Nut and nut butter- varied
Tofu- 11 grams per 4 oz.
Quinoa- 9 grams/cup
Legumes and grains- varied
Almonds-30 grams/cup
Flax seeds-31 grams/cup
Oat bran-7 grams/cup
Whole wheat bread-3 grams/oz.
Whole wheat spaghetti- 15 grams/cup

Gluten Free Vegan Proteins

Amaranth- 8 to 9 grams/cup
Quinoa-9 grams/cup
Brown rice-5 grams/cup
Legumes/beans/lentils-18 grams/cup
Kidney beans-16 grams/cup
Pecans-10 grams/cup
Almond flour-12 grams/cup
Pumpkin seeds-5 grams/oz.
Green vegetables-about 3 grams/cup
Fruit- contain small amount of protein
Rolled oats-6 grams/cup

To ensure you get the recommended daily allowance of protein, make sure you include a small amount in every meal and snack. This will help to keep you from slipping into a *junk-food-vegan-carbohydrate* mode.

Start your day by making a nutritious smoothie. Add rice or hemp powder to your smoothie and you'll get your protein for the morning. Another great way to make sure you get protein throughout the day is to make healthy snacks. Some ideas to get you started are to add roasted chickpeas or beans to your salad or pasta dish, snacking on hummus with veggies, and spreading nut butter on your morning toast, bagel, or apple.

Whole Grains

Whole Grains are an essential component of a vegan diet due to their high nutritional value and low fat content. A whole grain kernel has three parts:

Bran: The outer protective layer of the grain kernel, which has dietary fiber, antioxidants, minerals, and vitamins.

Germ: The smallest part of each kernel, the germ is the embryo of the kernel and is loaded with vitamins B and E, folate, healthy fats, antioxidants, minerals, and a bit of protein and fiber.

Endosperm: The largest part of the kernel, providing potential energy for the kernel to sprout and develop into a new plant. Endosperm is composed of *carbohydrates and protein.*

Types of Grains/Preparation

Couscous: Coucous is a small pasta made of semolina and is a good source of vegetarian protein. This whole grain food is native to Northern Africa and is commonly found in Middle Eastern cuisine. Eating this whole grain provides your body with essential nutrients to help maintain your overall health. It is a delicious replacement for rice in most dishes.

Cooking Directions: Bring 1 ½ cups water, (vegetable broth) to a boil. Add 1 cup couscous, cover and remove from heat. Let the couscous sit for 15 minutes or until all of the water is absorbed. Cover the pot, and let it rest for a few minutes. Fluff with a fork, and add salt if desired.

Faro: In addition to being rich in minerals and vitamins, faro contains large amounts of phytonutrients. Faro has twice the fiber and protein of modern wheat.

Cooking Directions: Rinse the faro in a fine mesh strainer for 1-2 minutes. Combine the faro with 2 ½ cups water. Bring to a boil, stir and reduce the heat to low. Simmer uncovered for 15-20 minutes, or until grains are tender. Drain off excess water, and add salt to taste.

Millet (*gluten free*): Millet is a good source of protein, vitamin B, and amino acids. It is low in fat and has no cholesterol. It also provides good bacteria that helps to maintain proper function of the intestines.

Cooking Directions: For a deeper flavor, toast 1 cup millet in a medium pot for 3-5 minutes. Add 2 cups water and bring to a boil. Reduce heat and simmer 25-30 minutes or until the millet is tender. Remove the pot from the heat, fluff with a fork, and let rest about 10 minutes before serving. Add salt to taste.

Quinoa (*gluten free*): This grain is considered a relative of green leafy vegetables such as swiss chard and spinach. Technically a seed, quinoa is rich in amino acids that are essential for maintaining overall body health. The texture is creamy, fluffy, and slightly crunchy with a nutty flavor.

Cooking Directions: Rinse the quinoa extremely well before cooking. Some packages will say it is not necessary to rinse the quinoa. It is still recommended that you do so to prevent the quinoa from tasting very bitter. In a medium pot, combine 1 cup quinoa with 2 cups water or vegetable broth. Bring to a boil, and then reduce heat. Cover and simmer 15-20 minutes, or until the liquid has been fully absorbed. Remove the pot from the heat and let rest, covered, for 10 minutes. Uncover, fluff with a fork, and add salt to taste.

Wheat Berries: Wheat berries are whole, unprocessed wheat kernels. In their most natural form, they contain protein, a lot of fiber, iron, calcium, vitamin B and E, folate and potassium. They are also low in fat.

Cooking Directions: Soak 1 cup wheat berries at least 8 hours, or overnight. Drain, combine with 4 cups water in a medium pot, and bring to a boil. Reduce the heat and simmer 1 hour or until tender. Drain off excess water, and add salt to taste.

Dried Beans

As a child growing-up in a small town near Birmingham, Alabama, we ate dried beans on a regular basis, usually with some type of smoked pork. Dried beans are cheap and offer a valuable source of micronutrients like iron, folate and magnesium. They are also easy to cook.

Before cooking beans, you should always pick through beans for small rocks, discolored beans, shriveled up beans, or debris. Rinse under cold water and soak beans 6-12 hours or overnight. The longer you soak beans, the faster they cook: the larger the beans, the longer they need to soak. The beans absorb water to dissolve the starches that cause intestinal discomfort. Soak 1 cup dried beans in 3 cups of cold water. If you are short on time and did not soak beans the night before, you can put rinsed beans in cold water and bring them to a gentle boil for 2 minutes. Take the beans off of the heat and allow beans to remain in water 1-2 hours. Drain and rinse the beans, and add fresh water to the cooking pot. Bring beans to a boil for a second time, reduce heat, add seasoning to taste and simmer for 1 to 1 ½ hours, or until tender. Beans are done when they can be mashed with a fork. Serve with brown rice to make a complete protein. Store cooked beans covered in the refrigerator for up to four days. Beans will last up to two months in a freezer.

Dairy

There are a number of non-dairy products you can make at home or purchase from most super markets. I'm not going to go into detail about how to make dairy free milk in this book but milks like almond milk, rice milk, and soy milk are generally available at most grocers. Health food stores usually carry a larger variety of non-dairy milks such as rice milk, hemp milk, all kinds of nut milk, coconut milk, and the list goes on.

Don't think for a minute that vegans miss out on the rich and luxurious taste of buttermilk just because we don't consume cow's milk.
To make buttermilk replacement in a recipe, add 1 Tbsp. vinegar per cup of

non-dairy milk.

Many people believe that the hardest part of becoming vegan is giving up cheese. While this is certainly debatable, there is no denying the delicious, creamy allure of a good soft cheese or the satisfaction of biting into a piece of sharp cheddar. Some vegan cheeses are available at your local supermarket or health food store. Daiya is largely regarded as the best, but it is still not a true alternative. There are many recipes available online for delicious homemade cheese and cheese sauces, some of which are quite delicious. Generally speaking, homemade "cheese" is your best option.

As for eggs, there are many vegan alternatives for cooking. To substitute one egg in a recipe, use one of the following:

- 1 Tbsp. milled flaxseed, plus 3 Tbsp. water blended (let sit 10-15 minutes)

- 1 Tbsp. soy flour, plus 1 Tbsp. of water, mix well with hand until blended.

- 1/4 cup mashed banana, plus 1/4 tsp. baking powder

- 1/4 cup apple sauce

- 1 Tbsp. white flour, plus ½ tsp. oil, plus 2 Tbsp. water, plus ½ Tbsp. baking powder.

- 2 Tbsp. arrowroot powder

- 2 Tbsp. corn starch, plus 3 Tbsp. water, blended.

- 1 Tbsp. whole flaxseed, plus 4 Tbsp. water, blended

Meat Substitutes

Sometimes, you might get the urge to chew on something a little more substantial. Luckily, there are a number of meat substitutes for vegans with a texture and flavor so close to meat that many carnivores don't know the difference.

Tofu: Tofu is high in protein, containing all of the essential amino acids. It is low in saturated fat with no cholesterol. Tofu can be enjoyed hot or cold, grilled, baked, stir-fried, or as a substitute for dairy, egg or meat. There are two kinds of tofu: processed and fresh. Tofu comes in Silken, Firm and Extra Firm. Use silken tofu for smoothies, soups and sauces. Use firm or extra-firm as a meat replacement. Tofu takes on the flavor of whatever you use to cook it. Therefore, it is easy to tailor it to your taste preferences.

Seitan: Seitan has been called wheat-meat or mock duck. It is made from the gluten in flour and can be made to taste like many kinds of meat. Seitan is especially great when making "sausage" or "hamburger." It is not difficult to make your own seitan at home.

Tempeh: Tempeh is a good source of protein and dietary fiber. It is made from fermented soybean and rice. Tempeh is different from tofu because it is made from the whole soybean, giving it a firm, meat-like texture.

There are a number of products made for vegans and vegetarians that can be used as meat replacement at your local super market including burgers, sausages, fake bacon, and more. Remember that just

because it is vegetarian does not mean it is dairy-free. Please read the
label to make sure it says "vegan."

The Fantastic Super Food: Seeds

Sesame Seeds: Sesame seeds come in many different colors: red, black, yellow, several shades of brown, and most commonly, a pale white-gray. The darker seeds have a richer flavor. Be careful to avoid any seeds that have been dyed. Sesame seeds are usually sold in two varieties: hulled and un-hulled. Hulled seeds have been stripped of their dry outer covering. This is the type of seed you find on a hamburger bun. Un-hulled seeds are referred to as 'natural' sesame seeds. Because of their high oil content, sesame seeds spoil easily. If not refrigerated, they should be kept in a cool dry place like an airtight container. This way they can last up to three months. If refrigerated or frozen, they can last for up to a year. Sesame seeds are beneficial to the heart and nervous system thanks to their high vitamin E content.

How Are Sesame Seeds Used?

Sesame seeds are a prominent ingredient in Asian dishes. The seeds can also be used to make bread, crackers, tahini, and smoothies, and they can be added to sweet or savory dishes.

Pumpkin Seeds: Pumpkin seeds are a *heart healthy* snack. Pumpkin seeds contains magnesium, which is essential for a healthy heart. They provide omega-3 and omega-6 fatty acids. The addition of these fatty acids to the diet has been found to increase energy, mental health, and overall vitality. For a good night's sleep, have your pumpkin seeds a few hours before bed. They contain the amino acid tryptophan, the same stuff that makes Thanksgiving Turkey such a stupor-inducing meal. They also boost the production of your serotonin levels and promote a restful night's sleep.

How Are Pumpkin Seeds Used?

Pumpkin seed shells are an excellent source of dietary fiber. To dry pumpkin seeds quickly, spread them in a single layer on a baking sheet, and bake them at 250 degrees for about 20 minutes. After 20 minutes, toss them with oil and the spices of your choice. Return them to the oven for another 20 minutes.

Alternatively, you can spread the seeds on a sheet of parchment paper, and use a rolling pin to crack the shell. Add seeds to a pot of boiling water (the cracked shells will open and release their kernels). Discard the shells, rinse the kernels, and let them air dry. Store in an airtight container in the refrigerator. They will keep for six months in the refrigerator.

Chia Seeds: Chia seeds come from a flowering plant in the mint family that's native to Mexico and Guatemala. History suggests it was a very important crop for the Aztecs. It has remained in regular use in its native countries, but was largely unknown in North American until researcher Wayne Coats begin studying chia as an alternative crop for farmers in northern Argentina a few years ago. Coats started his work on chia in 1991. Since then, he then has become an advocate of the tiny seed's health benefits. The human trials are limited- as is often the case with food research- but the anecdotal evidence of chia's positive health effects include boosting energy, stabilizing blood sugar, aiding digestion, and lowering cholesterol.

The little seed, which comes in either white, dark brown, or black, also has a huge nutritional profile. It contains calcium, manganese, and phosphorus and is a great source of healthy omega-3 fats. As an added benefit, chia seeds can be eaten whole or milled.

How Are Chia Seeds Used?

Chia seeds can be added to the diet in a variety of ways. The most common uses are to make a chia-seed pudding or sprinkle whole seeds on top of salads, toast, or cereal. They can also be added whole or milled to smoothies or ice cream, and they can be added to water with lemon juice, sweetener, and flavoring to make a refreshing drink.

Hemp Seeds: While the hemp plant may look like marijuana, it is actually a different species of cannabis and contains very little of the active ingredient THC (delta-9-tetra-hydro-cannabis) that gives marijuana its reputation. Hemp seeds provide a good vegetarian source of omega-3 fatty acids, which are essential fats that help reduce inflammation and may reduce the risk of heart disease. Hemp seeds may also help lower cholesterol and blood pressure. Omega-3 fatty acids are found in concentrated amounts in the brain and may play an important role in helping memory and cognitive function.

How Are Hemp Seeds Used?

Hemp seeds can be used to make hemp milk and hemp flour. They can be added to hot cereal, yogurt or smoothies. Sprinkle hemp seeds over salads, pudding, and oatmeal. It can also be used for baking and cooking.

Kitchen supplies

Having the right appliances in the kitchen, can increase the number and variety of recipes you are able to prepare, and also decrease the time it takes to prepare them. You should also increase your knowledge of vegan substitutes so that you can prepare food to taste as close to your favorite foods as possible.

Good Knives: Invest in at least three good knives. You will enjoy cooking so much more when you have a variety of high-quality knives that feel good in your hands.
1- Chef's knife with a 7-9 inch blade
2- Paring knife with a 3-4 inch blade
3- Serrated knife with a 9-10 inch blade

Two Wooden Cutting Boards: Use one cutting board for onion and garlic *only*. Due to limited storage space in my kitchen, I have one wooden cutting board and use both sides: one side for onion and garlic and the other side for everything else

Coffee/Spice grinder: It takes very little time to grind your own spices, and you'll taste the different in the flavors immediately. Note: if you are using flax-seed as an egg replacement in baking, you *must* use freshly ground flax seeds.

Cast Iron Skillet: Cast iron is affordable and lasts forever. It provides a bit of iron in your food. Cast iron is the most convenient type of skillet because you can pop it in the oven if necessary.

Food Processor: A food processor can be used to slice, dice, chop, or puree food. It is one of the most regularly used appliances in a vegan kitchen. Choose one with a decent size bowl. I have a Kitchen Aid, and I use it frequently.

Blender: Blenders can emulsify or puree foods. Having a high-speed blender in your kitchen can insure you can make your own wholesome smoothies at home with your favorite fruits and vegetables. This allows you to retain the original dietary fiber content in whatever special combination you desire.

Immersion Blender: Immersion blenders are good for blending hot soups or smoothies.

Salad spinner: The salad spinner makes it easy to get most of the water off of salad greens. After I began eating a plant-based diet, my consumption of salad greens increased dramatically.

Juicer: One of the main benefits of juicing is that it makes the nutrients in fruit and vegetable more easy for the body to absorb.

Part Two

Smoothies

Part Two

Smoothies are a good way to get your recommended daily intake of fresh fruit and vegetables. They are so easy to prepare! Just put everything in a blender, and you have a complete meal that tastes delicious without have to spend hours in the kitchen. You can sneak in some leafy-green vegetables with your fresh fruit, add nut-butter (or nuts) and non-dairy milk or water. Yum

Recipes in This Section

Kale and Collard Greens Smoothie
Blueberry Smoothie
Mama Suebee's Ginger Banana Smoothie
Pina-Colada Smoothie
Feel Good Smoothie
Super-Food Green Smoothie
Green Apple Smoothie
Strawberry 'Cheese' Cake Smoothie

Kale and Collard Energy Smoothie

Ingredients
2 kale leaves, stems removed
2 collard leaves, stems removed
1 apple, core removed
2 carrots
1 cup strawberries, frozen
1 ripe banana
1 Tbsp. fresh lemon juice
Pinch of Celtic sea salt
4-5 ice cubes, optional

Yield: 1 Serving
Serving Size: About 2 cups

Place the kale, collards, apple,
carrots, strawberries and banana in a high-

power blender. Blend until smooth. Add lemon juice, salt and ice cubes. Pulse to combine. Transfer to a glass. Enjoy!

Pina Colada Smoothie

<u>Ingredients</u>
½ cup organic pineapple juice
½ cup raw coconut milk
1 cup pineapple chunks, frozen
4 ice cubes

Yield: 1 Serving
Serving Size: About 1 ½ cups

Blend pineapple juice, coconut milk and pineapple chunks in high speed blender, and puree until smooth and frosty. Add ice cubes and blend 15 seconds more. Pour in Mason jar or glass. Garnish with pineapple slices. Enjoy!

Note: Fresh pineapple is low in

calories and is an excellent source of antioxidants and vitamin C. Pineapples are also rich in B complex and minerals. In this smoothie, it is used as a flavoring ingredient.

Super-Food Green Smoothie

<u>Ingredients</u>
2 large handful of your favorite greens , I
use Kale and Collards
1 large handful of spinach, bok choy, or
chard
¼ cup blueberries
1 cup grapes, seeded and rinsed
2 cups distilled water
1 tsp. maca, *optional*
¼ cup goji berries, *optional*
1 tsp. barley grass powder, *optional*
2 Tbsp. lemon juice, *optional*
1/8 tsp. Celtic sea salt, *optional*

Yield: 2 Servings
Serving Size: About 2 cups

Place all ingredients in a blender, and puree for about 1 minute on high. Add ½ to 1 cup crushed ice if you prefer a frosty cold smoothie. Pour into two 16 oz. size mason jars or large glasses, and garnish with mint sprigs if desired. Enjoy!

Green Apple Smoothie
(Like Grandma's apple pie with ice cream!)

<u>Ingredients</u>
½ cup unsweetened unpasteurized apple juice
½ cup distilled water
1 Tbsp. cashew nuts
½ tsp. ground cinnamon
¼ tsp. vanilla extract
1/8 tsp. ground nutmeg
½ English cucumber
2 cups spinach
1 apple, chopped and frozen
6 ice cubes

Yield: 2 Servings
Serving Size: About 1 ½ cups

Add all ingredients to a high speed blender, then puree for about 40 seconds or until smooth. Pour into 16 oz. mason jars. Enjoy.

Strawberry Cheese Cake Smoothie

This smoothie is incredibly simple to prepare and tastes like real cheesecake: thick, rich and oh so yummy. This is a favorite holiday drink in our family, though we have it anytime, and so can you.

Ingredients
1 cup strawberries, fresh or frozen
1 cup non-dairy milk , I use vanilla almond milk
3 Tbsp. gluten-free oats
1 Tbsp. chia seeds
1 Tbsp. cashew nuts
1 tsp. apple cider vinegar
1 tsp. fresh lemon juice
½ tsp. pure vanilla extract

1 serving sweetener of your choice, I use agave nectar

Yield: 1 Serving
Serving Size: About 2 cups

Make the night before or 4 hours in advance of serving. Stir all ingredients into a 24-oz. mason jar and refrigerate. Just before serving, pour ingredients into a blender, and process until smooth. Enjoy!

Blueberry Smoothie

Blueberries claim to be a nutritional powerhouse, and are among the healthiest food choices. The antioxidants in blueberries help prevent cancer and lower the risk of cardiovascular disease. Blueberries can also help to preserve younger looking skin and can help reduce skin sagging.

<u>Ingredients</u>
¾ cup ice cold non-dairy milk
2/3 cup frozen blueberries
2 Tbsp. vanilla rice protein powder
1 serving sweetener of your choice (*stevia, agave nectar, honey, or maple syrup)*
5-7 ice cubes

Yield: 1 Serving
Serving Size: About 2 cups

Combine the milk and blueberries in a high-powered blender, and blend until smooth. Add remaining ingredients, and blend until well combined. Add ice cubes, and pulse 2 times. Pour the smoothie into a glass or Mason jar. Enjoy

Mama Suebee Ginger Banana Shake

Bananas are an excellent source of B-6 and are easy to digest. They can be an appealing way to get some important nutrients into your system without upsetting your stomach. Ginger is known primarily for its detoxification benefits. It may also help to promote healthy digestion.

Ingredients
2 cups ripe banana
2 cups carrots
1 medium beet, peeled and cut into chunks
¼ cup lemon juice
2 oranges, peeled, with seeds removed
1/3 cup agave nectar
1/3 cup dried plums
4 celery stalks, cut into 2 inch pieces

2 inches fresh ginger peeled
2 cups distilled water
3 Tbsp. Barley Max, *optional*
1 Tbsp. Trio, *optional*
2 Tbsp. Chia seeds, *optional*
½ tsp. sea salt, *optional*

Yield: 4 Servings
Serving Size: 2 cups/16 oz.

Place all ingredients in a blender, and mix until everything is pureed. Enjoy!

Feel Good Smoothie

The hemp seeds in this smoothie, are one way to get a good dose of plant-based protein and all kinds of essential vitamins, minerals and essential fatty acids. The maca powder will increase your energy level and endurance.

Ingredients
1 banana, frozen
½ cup blueberries, frozen
2 Tbsp. hemp seeds
1 tsp. maca powder
1 tsp. omega 3, 6, 9 oil
1 ½ cup distilled water
1 scoop raw vegan protein powder

Yield: 1 Serving
Serving Size: About 2 cups

Blend all ingredients until smooth. Enjoy!

Part Three

Hummus

Part Three

Hummus is a staple in most vegan/vegetarian refrigerators. It is so easy to make and will keep for 5-6 days. Hummus can be eaten as a dip with pita bread, crackers, or fresh vegetables, and can be easily added to wraps and sandwiches. The garbanzo beans are packed with protein, iron, and fiber, making them especially important for vegans.

Recipes in This Section

Roasted Red Pepper Hummus
Cucumber Hummus
Butternut Squash Hummus
Lemon Artichoke Hummus
Green Olive Hummus
White Beans and Roasted Egg Plant Hummus

Roasted Red Pepper Hummus

Red bell peppers are amazingly sweet, compared to green, yellow or orange bell peppers. Bell peppers are a good source of vitamin A, potassium and antioxidants, including lutein, which help protect against sight loss, bell pepper is a very important contribution to the vegan/vegetarian diet, adding color, crunch and flavor, without the calories.

Ingredients
1 (15 oz.) can chickpeas (garbanzo beans) rinsed and drained
2 Tbsp., or 1 fresh lemon juiced
2 Tbsp. tahini, sesame paste
3 cloves fresh garlic, peeled and chopped coarsely
1/3 cup roasted red peppers
3 Tbsp. extra virgin olive oil
2 Tbsp. fresh basil roughly chopped
½ tsp. Celtic sea salt

Pinch cayenne pepper, optional
1 tsp. cumin, optional

Yield: 4 Servings
Serving Size: About 1/3 cup

Place garlic in food processor, and blend on high until the garlic sticks to the sides of the bowl. Scrape down bowl, and add fresh lemon juice and tahini. Process on high until juice and tahini is thick and creamy. Combine chickpeas, red pepper, olive oil, fresh basil, salt and pepper in food processor until smooth. Transfer hummus to a bowl or glass container, and refrigerate 1-2 hours or until chilled. Enjoy!

Cucumber Hummus

This Hummus is a good appetizer to start any meal, while waiting for your meal at a restaurant or home- cooking. My husband doesn't like regular hummus. But when I serve this, he asks for seconds!

Ingredients
1 cup diced cucumbers
2 cloves garlic
1 Tbsp. distilled water
1 tsp. flax-seed, ground
1 (15 oz.) can chickpeas, or 1 ½ cups, rinsed and drained
1 Tbsp. tahini
2 Tbsp. lemon juice
½ tsp. Celtic sea salt, or to taste
¼ tsp. sumac, optional for garnish

Yield: 6 Servings
Serving Size: About 1/3 cup

Put the cucumber, water, garlic, and flax-seed into a blender or food processor and blend on high speed until frothy. Add the remaining ingredients (except sumac), and blend on high until smooth. Pour hummus unto a bowl or glass container, and refrigerate 2 hours or until chilled and slightly thicker. Sprinkle with sumac and serve. Enjoy!

Classic Butternut Squash Hummus

Butternut squash is a rich source of vitamin A, and like other winter squash, it also provides fiber. When choosing a winter squash, always find one that is rock solid with the stem attached. If the stem is missing, beware. The opening that is left can allow bacteria to enter and spoil the flesh.

Ingredients
2 ½ cups butternut squash, peeled and cubed
1/4 cup extra virgin olive oil
1 tsp. smoked paprika
1/4 tsp. dried oregano
1 Tbsp. raw honey
1 (15) oz. can chickpeas
2 Tbsp. tahini
3 Tbsp. fresh lemon juice

2 clove garlic, minced

½ tsp. cinnamon
½ tsp. pumpkin pie spice
½ tsp. Celtic sea salt
Cayenne pepper to taste

Yield: 8 Servings
Serving Size: About ½ cup

Preheat oven to 400 F. In medium bowl, toss butternut squash with 2 Tbsp. olive oil, paprika, oregano, honey, salt and pepper. Arrange squash on baking sheet in a single layer. Roast squash 25 minutes, or until tender. Allow squash to cool and add to food processor, along with remaining ingredients, puree until desired consistency is reached. Transfer hummus to a bowl. Store hummus in refrigerator, for up to 5 days. Enjoy!

Lemon Artichoke Hummus

This traditional hummus is spiced up by adding artichoke hearts. It has a light texture and tastes magnificent with pita bread or crackers. Adjust the spices to your taste.

<u>Ingredients</u>
1 cup canned artichoke hearts, rinsed, dried and chopped
2 lemons juiced, or 4 Tbsp.
¼ cup water
5 Tbsp. tahini, stirred well
2 Tbsp. olive oil, + extra for drizzling
1 (15 oz.) can chickpeas, drained and rinsed
1 clove garlic, minced
½ tsp. Celtic sea salt
¼ tsp. lemon zest
½ tsp. cayenne pepper, optional
2 tsp. fresh parsley

Yield: 8 Servings
Serving Size: About 1/3 cup

Set aside ¼ cup of the artichokes for garnish. In a small bowl, combine the water and lemon juice. In another bowl, whisk the tahini and olive oil together. In a food processor, blend the chickpeas, ¾ cup artichokes, garlic, salt, ¼ tsp. cayenne pepper, and lemon zest. Pulse for about 15 seconds. Use a spatula to scrape ingredients off the sides of the bowl. Turn the processor on and add the lemon water slowly through the top. Scrape the sides again and continue to blend about 1 minute. Again turn the processor on, slowly add the tahini/oil mixture, and process until smooth (about 15 seconds). Continue to scrape the sides of the bowl. Place the hummus into a bowl and garnish with the extra artichokes, parsley, and ¼ tsp. cayenne pepper. Let stand at least 15 minutes, then drizzle with olive oil before serving. Enjoy!

Green Olive Hummus

<u>Ingredients</u>
3 large cloves garlic
2 cans, or 3 cups chickpeas, rinsed and
drained if using canned
Juice of 1 lemon
½ cup green olives, stuffed with pimentos
2 Tbsp. vegetable broth
1 Tbsp. tahini
1/8 tsp. cayenne pepper
½ tsp. Celtic sea salt
6-7 more olives

Yield: 12 Servings
Serving Size: About 1/3 cup

　　　Place garlic cloves in food processor
and pulse until garlic is well chopped. Add
the chickpeas and lemon juice and

coarsely chop. Add the green olives, vegetable broth, tahini, and seasonings. Process until everything is mixed well. Salt to taste, then add the remaining 6-7 olives. Pulse a few times just to barely chop the olives. Transfer hummus to a bowl or glass container and refrigerate one hour or overnight. Enjoy!

White Beans and Roasted Eggplant Hummus

Eggplant is one of my favorite meat replacing vegetables. Like the avocado and tomato, this member of the nightshade family is actually a fruit (specifically a berry) but is usually treated like a vegetable.

1 ½ pounds eggplant, or 3 Japanese eggplants, trimmed and cut into 2 inch pieces.
1/3 cup extra virgin olive oil + more for drizzling
½ tsp. fresh ground black pepper
½ tsp. Celtic sea salt, plus more for seasoning
1 (15 oz.) can cannellini beans, rinsed and drained

1/3 cup flat leaf parsley
¼ cup fresh lemon juice
¼ cup tahini
3 cloves garlic
2 tsp. cumin
1 tsp. red chili flakes
1 tsp. smoked paprika
1 English cucumber, cut into 1/4 inch
thick slices, for garnish

Yield: 8 Servings
Serving Size: About 1/3 cup
     Place an oven rack in the middle of
the oven, and preheat to 450 degrees F.
Place the eggplant on a baking sheet lined
with parchment paper. Drizzle with olive
oil (saving 1/3 cup) and season with salt
and pepper. Roast for 25 minutes until
golden brown, then set aside to cool. In the
bowl of the food processor, combine the
cooled eggplant and all other ingredients
(except cucumbers). Serve with sliced
cucumber. Enjoy!

Part Four

Main Meals and Side Dishes

Part Four

Recipes in This Section

Not My Mama's Tuna
Cauliflower Macaroni and 'Cheese'
Favorite Nigerian Black-eyed Peas
Kale, Tomatoes and Chickpeas
Spaghetti Squash with spicy Braised Greens
Spiced Kale and White Beans
White Button Mushroom 'Meat Balls'
Cabbage, Bell Pepper and Onion
Black-Eyed Peas 'Picked'
Singapore Slaw
Brown Rice Pudding
Sweet Potato Pone-Pone
Pineapple Cornbread Muffins
Sweet Potato Tart with Pecan Crust
Honey Roasted Candied Walnuts

Banana Bread Cookies
Cashew Milk, Vanilla

Not My Mama's "Tuna"

This salad is simple and light, yet satisfying. Make 1 hour before serving, so the flavors can marinate.

Ingredients
2 cups organic chickpeas, rinsed and drained
1 cup plus 2 Tbsp. Vegenaise
1 medium red onion, chopped
3/4 cup celery, chopped
½ cup dill pickle spears, chopped
1 Tbsp. brown or yellow mustard
1 tsp. apple cider vinegar
¾ tsp. celery salt
Pepper to taste
½ tsp. smoked paprika
1 tsp. kelp powder
2 Tbsp. nutritional yeast

Bread of your choice

Yield: 6 Servings
Serving Size: About 1 sandwich

Place chickpeas in food processor, and pulse several times. Be careful not to completely pulverize the chickpeas. The goal is to break them down to a texture similar to tuna. Transfer to a large bowl, and add nutritional yeast, onions, celery and pickles. Stir well. Next, stir in Vegenaise, mustard and vinegar. Season with, celery salt, pepper, paprika, and kelp. Mix again, can be eaten with crackers, on a sandwich, or any way you eat tuna. Enjoy!

Favorite Nigerian Black-Eyed Peas

In the Southern United States, black-eyed peas are prepared with ham hocks and rice. Black-eyed peas are rich in fiber, and are a good source of folate, potassium, copper, phosphorous, and manganese.

Ingredients
2 cups black-eyed peas, soaked overnight
1 tsp. Celtic sea salt
½ tsp. black pepper
1/4 cup grapeseed oil

Yield: 12 Servings
Serving Size: About 2-3 balls

Soak the black-eyed peas overnight. Drain excess water from peas. In a blender add black-eyed peas, Celtic sea salt and black pepper, mix until beans become a paste, but still a bit course, add water if needed to make smooth paste. Heat grape-seed oil in frying pan. When oil is hot, scoop one spoonful of paste into hot oil, repeat until frying pan is full, turn occasionally and remove from oil when brownish in color. Serve with your favorite sauce. Enjoy!

Kale, Tomatoes and Chickpeas

This simple entree turns kale into a special treat, especially in the summer when tomatoes are extra sweet and readily available.

2 Tbsp. grapeseed oil
1 yellow onion, peeled and diced
4 garlic cloves, peeled and sliced
1/8 tsp. chili flakes
¼ tsp. Celtic sea salt
2 Tbsp. smoked paprika
2 tsp. cumin
2 large tomatoes, chopped
2 cups vegetable broth
1 bunch kale, washed and stems removed
1 (15oz.) can chickpeas, drained and rinsed
Small hand full of fresh basil

2 tsp. extra virgin olive oil, to drizzle on top

Yield: 4 Servings
Serving Size: About 3/4 cup

Heat oil in large, heavy pot. Set over medium-high heat. Add onion, garlic, chili, and salt. Cook, stirring occasionally, until softened (about 10 minutes). Meanwhile, chop the kale, and remove the bitter stems. Stir in tomato along with 2 cups vegetable broth and kale. Bring stew to a boil, lower the heat, and simmer for 35 minutes. Add beans during the last 10 minutes of cooking. The kale should be completely soft. Serve each portion with a drizzle of extra virgin olive oil and a few basil leaves torn over the top. Enjoy!

Cauliflower Macaroni and 'Cheese'

I use whole wheat pasta in this dish. Pureed cauliflower make this sauce so silky smooth, even carnivores love it and ask for seconds!

<u>Ingredients</u>
½ lb. dry macaroni pasta, cooked according to package instructions
1 cup cooked and smashed cauliflower (about ½ cauliflower)
1 large carrot, peeled and cut into 1 inch pieces
¼ cup nutritional yeast flakes
¼ cup extra virgin olive oil
3 Tbsp. water
2 tsp. lemon juice
1 tsp. Celtic sea salt, or to taste
¼ cup bread crumbs, optional

Yield: 3 Servings
Serving Size: About 3/4 cup

Cook pasta according to package directions, drain, and set aside. In a large pot, bring 3-4 cups water to a boil. Cut the florets off of the cauliflower. Peel and cut your carrots. Place cauliflower florets and carrots in the boiling water, and cook for about 15-17 minutes (or until cauliflower is soft enough to be mashed with a fork). Remove vegetables from pot, and drain off excess water. Mash cauliflower with a fork, and place 1 packed cup of mashed cauliflower in food processor. Add carrots, oil, water, lemon juice, yeast flakes, and seasonings to your food processor and process until smooth and creamy. Pour cooked pasta into a medium pot or bowl. Pour all of your "cheese" mixture over your pasta and gently fold it together. Sprinkle bread crumbs on top of macaroni and "cheese" and serve. Enjoy!

Spaghetti Squash with Spicy Braised Greens

Spaghetti squash contains folic acid, potassium, vitamin A and beta carotene. It is also low in calories, averaging 42 calories per 1 cup serving. Some leafy greens also contain beta carotene, such as collards greens, spinach and swiss chard

<u>ingredients</u>
1 small spaghetti squash, halved lengthwise, seeds removed
2 Tbsp. coconut oil
2 garlic cloves, minced
2 chipotle chilies, canned in adobo, seeded and minced

1 large bunch (12 to 16 ounces) kale, chard, or collard greens, thick ribs removed, leaves sliced crosswise
1 cup vegetable broth
3/4 tsp. Celtic sea salt
1/4 cup raisins
1/4 cup pine nuts, toasted
2 Tbsp. olive oil

Yield: 6 Servings
Serving Size: About 3/4 cup

Preheat oven to 375 degrees. Place squash cut-side down in a roasting pan. Pour in 1/4 inch water and bake 50 minutes. Heat coconut oil in a large pot over medium heat. Add garlic and chipotle and cook, stirring constantly for 1 minute. Add greens a few handful at a time, stirring between additions. Add broth, ½ tsp. salt, and raisins. Bring to a boil and cover. Lower heat and simmer 20 minutes or until greens are tender. Stir in 3 Tbsp.

pine nuts. When squash is done, use a metal spoon to scoop flesh out into a bowl, separating into strands. Add olive oil and remaining 1/4 tsp. salt and toss gently. Transfer to a serving dish, top with greens, and serve. Garnish with remaining pine nuts. Enjoy!

Spiced Kale and White Beans

White beans are a good source of protein and dietary fiber. And they are full of vitamins and minerals.

Ingredients
1 Tbsp. grapeseed oil
3 cloves garlic cloves, minced
4 scallions, sliced
1 ½ lb. kale, ribs removed and coarsely chopped
1 cup vegetable broth, low sodium
1 Tbsp. tandoori marsala
¼ tsp. Celtic sea salt
1 (15oz.) can of white beans

Yield: 4 Servings

Serving Size: About ¾ cup

Heat oil in Dutch oven over medium heat. Add garlic and scallions, and cook, stirring until fragrant, for about 30 sec. Add kale and cook, tossing with 2 large spoons, until bright green (about 1 minute). Add broth, marsala, and salt. Cover and cook until kale is tender (8-10 minutes). Stir in beans, cover, and cook until beans are heated throughout (about 1-2 min). Serve over spaghetti squash, with baked potato, or as a side dish. Enjoy!

Cabbage with Bell Pepper and Onion

If you are tired of boring cabbage, try out this cruciferous vegetable with a zesty flavor. The red and green peppers make this dish as visually pleasing, as it is delicious.

<u>Ingredients</u>
1 medium green cabbage, about 2 pounds
½ red bell pepper, sliced
½ green bell pepper, sliced
1 large red onion, sliced
2 Tbsp. extra virgin olive oil
¼ cup vegetable broth
2 ears fresh corn, cut from cob, or ½ cup
2 carrots, sliced
1 tsp. garlic powder
1 tsp. Celtic sea salt
½ tsp. freshly ground black pepper

Yield: 6-8 Servings

Serving Size: About ½ cup

Cut the cabbage in half, and remove the center core. Dice the core (except the thick stem end), and thinly slice the remaining cabbage. Set to the side. In a large saucepan, heat the oil over medium heat. Stir in the onions and bell pepper. Cook for 6-8 minutes or until peppers and onion are soft. Stir in the vegetable broth. Add the carrots, corn, cabbage, garlic powder, salt, and pepper. Bring to a boil, reduce heat, and simmer 20 minutes or until cabbage is tender. Remove from heat and let rest 15 minutes before serving. Enjoy!

Brown Rice Pudding

Our food ranking system qualified brown rice as an excellent source of manganese and a good source of selenium, phosphorus, copper, magnesium, and niacin (Vitamin B-3). The complete milling polishing that converts brown rice into white rice destroys 67% of the vitamin B3, 80% of the vitamin B1, 90% of the vitamin B6, 50% of the manganese, 50% of the phosphorus, 60% of the iron, and 100% of the dietary fiber and essential fatty acids. Moral of the story: stick with brown rice.

Ingredients
2 cups brown rice (regular, not long grain), cooked
1 (½) cups vanilla almond milk
1 tsp. vanilla extract
½ tsp. cinnamon

2 Tbsp. maple syrup
3 Tbsp. organic raisins
1 Tbsp. coconut oil

Preheat oven to 350-degrees F. Mix all ingredients in a medium baking dish, and stir until well incorporated. Put dish in oven, and cook pudding with dish uncovered about 20 minutes, stirring occasionally, until pudding begin to thicken a little. It can be served hot or cold. Enjoy!

Sweet Potato Pone-Pone

Sweet potatoes are readily available, inexpensive, and delicious. They are high in Vitamins B6 and C, and also contain Vitamin D, Iron, Magnesium, and Potassium. They are naturally sweet tasting.

<u>Ingredients</u>
2 medium sweet potatoes, grated
1 cup molasses
2 tsp. ground ginger
2 tsp. baking powder
1 tsp. Celtic sea salt
1/3 cup grapeseed oil

Yield: 8 Servings
Serving Size: About ½ cup

Combine all ingredients in a 3-quart saucepan and simmer slowly, stirring constantly, for about 10 minutes. Pour into well-greased 8x8 inch baking dish. Bake at 325 degrees F for 30 minutes, stirring every 5 minutes for the first 20 minutes. Smooth down the top, and allow to brown. Cut into squares, and serve either hot or cold. Enjoy!

Pineapple Cornbread Muffins

I grew up loving cornbread and sweets (syrup, jellies, jam, etc.), so creating this recipes was a no brainer for me. The taste reminds me of my childhood with family and friends gathered around a big table with lots of good food.

<u>Ingredients</u>
½ cup organic cornmeal
½ cup whole wheat pastry flour
¼ tsp. Celtic sea salt
¾ tsp. baking soda
1 cup crushed pineapple, in its own juice
¼ cup applesauce, unsweetened
¼ cup distilled water
½ cup agave nectar
Non-stick cooking spray

Yield: 18 Servings
Serving Size: About 1 muffin

Preheat oven to 350-degrees F. Stir together the dry ingredients in a large bowl. In a second bowl, stir together the wet ingredients. Once both bowls are mixed completely, combine them together until everything is moist. Spoon into lightly oiled muffin tins until they're 3/4 full. Bake for 25-30 minutes or until an inserted toothpick comes out clean. Enjoy!

Sweet Potato Tart with Pecan Crust

Pecans are an excellent source of vitamin E, riboflavin, niacin, thiamin, vitamin B6 and folate. The nuts are also a rich source of minerals like manganese, potassium, iron, magnesium, zinc, and selenium.

Ingredients

¾ cup pecan halves
¾ cup rolled oats
¾ cup whole wheat pastry flour
½ tsp. ground cinnamon
1/8 tsp. Celtic sea salt
¼ cup apple sauce, unsweetened
½ cup plus 3Tbsp pure maple syrup
1 cup cashew milk, or non-dairy milk of choice
¼ cup arrow root powder
1 medium sweet potato, baked and peeled
1 Tbsp. grated fresh ginger
1 ½ tsp. ground cinnamon

½ tsp. nutmeg
1/8 tsp. ground cloves
½ tsp. Celtic sea salt

Yield: 8 Servings
Serving Size: About 1 slice

Preheat the oven to 375 degrees F. Spray a 9" pie plate with non-stick cooking spray. Spread nuts over a baking pan. Toast for 8-10 minutes. Set aside 16 pecans for garnish. Combine oats, flour, remaining pecans, ½ tsp. cinnamon, and a pinch of salt in a food processor. Pulse until mixture becomes a coarse meal. Whisk together oil and 3 Tbsp. maple syrup, and mix into dry ingredients to form a soft dough.

Press mixture into pie plate. Bake for 10 minutes and set aside to cool. Blend milk and arrowroot in the food processor until the arrowroot is completely dissolved and the texture is smooth (about 12 seconds). Add potatoes, ½ cup maple syrup, ginger, 1 ½ tsp. nutmeg, and cloves; blend until smooth. Pour filling into crust and smooth the top. Bake for about 35 minutes or until crust is lightly browned and the outside inch of the filling is set. Transfer pie to a wire rack. Gently press toasted pecan halves into hot filling in 2 circles. Cool to room temperature, and then chill until set (about 3 hours). Serve chilled or at room temperature. Enjoy!

Honey Roasted Candied Walnuts

These nuts are ideal to serve at your next family gathering or house party. Walnuts are known to lower cholesterol, reduce the risk of heart disease, and decrease inflammation.

Ingredients
1 cup chopped walnuts
2 Tbsp. raw honey
1/3 tsp. cayenne pepper
1/8 tsp. Celtic sea salt

Yield: 8 Servings
Serving Size: About 2 Tbsp.

Preheat oven to 350-degrees F. Line cookie sheet with parchment paper and set aside. Put honey, cayenne, and salt in medium pot over low heat. Stir and heat until honey has thinned.

Remove the mixture from heat, and pour the walnuts into the pot. Mix with a large spoon until all nuts are covered with mixture. Spread nut mixture on cookie sheet and bake for 15 minutes. Stir nuts around halfway through baking time. Once nuts have cooled, place them in a sealed container to enjoy anytime.

Banana Bread Cookies

A banana has about 110 calories, is fat and cholesterol free, and can be substituted for some of the butter or oil when baking. A banana contains over 400 mg. potassium. Potassium helps maintain a healthy balance of fluids in the body and is necessary for good nerve and muscle function. The potassium in bananas can help prevent muscle cramps after exercise.

<u>Ingredients</u>
2 large ripe bananas
½ cup pitted Medjool dates
¼ cup extra virgin coconut oil
1 tsp. pure vanilla extract
1 tsp. cinnamon
1 tsp. Rumford baking powder
½ tsp. Celtic sea salt

2 cups organic rolled oats
¼ cup pecans, optional
¼ cup unsweet coconut

Yield: 16 Servings
Serving Size: About 2 cookies

Preheat oven to 350 degrees F. Line a large baking sheet with parchment paper. Add peeled bananas, coconut oil, pitted dates, and vanilla to food processor; process until well blended. Add baking powder, cinnamon, and salt; process until well combined. Add 1 ½ cups of the rolled oats, and pulse 4 seconds more.

Transfer to a medium bowl, and stir in the remaining ½ cup rolled oats, pecans, and coconut. Using a small scoop, put dough on parchment paper, and press down on the dough to flatten. Bake for 7 minutes. Remove cookies and place on cooling rack for 15 minutes.

Vanilla Cashew Milk

Making your own non-dairy milk at home is easier than you might think. It can be a fantastic way to experiment with new flavors. Add pumpkin pie spice (or your favorite spices) for a real treat.

Ingredients
1 cup raw cashews
3 cups distilled water
2 Tbsp. raw honey
½ tsp. vanilla bean powder
1/8 tsp. almond extract
1 tsp. cinnamon
Pinch of Celtic sea salt

Yield: 4 Servings
Serving Size: About 1 cup

Add all ingredients to high speed blender, and blend until silky smooth with a texture similar to milk. Voila! Milk will keep well in the refrigerator for up to 5 days. Shake well before using. Enjoy!

Part Five

Raw and Dehydrated

Part Five

Recipes in This Section

Nutty Berries
Raw Carrot Cake
Raw Cashew Cookies
Raw Cream 'Cheese' Frosting
Raw Oatmeal Fudge
Blueberries and Cream Kale Chips
Carrot Pulp Bread
'Cheesy' Kale Chips
Easy Super-Food Chia Seed Pudding
Home-Made Corn Chips
Irresistible Ice Cream
Home-Made Tomato Powder
'Salmon' Pate
Chia Seed Pudding with Coconut
Raw Sweet Kale Soup

Nutty Berries

<u>Ingredients</u>
3 cups almonds, soaked 1 hour
3 cups walnuts, soaked 1 hour
¾ cup blue berries
¾ cup black berries
¾ cup strawberries
3 Tbsp. maple syrup

Yield: 8 Servings
Serving Size: About ¾ cup

In a blender combine blueberries, blackberries, strawberries, and maple syrup, and blend until smooth. Pour mixture in bowl of almonds and walnuts, and stir until nuts are well coated. Place on Excalibur Parrflex sheet, and dehydrate at 105 degrees F for 10-12 hours or until dry. Enjoy!

Raw Carrot Cake

This is my family's favorite desert. Carrots are perhaps best known for their beta carotene content. They are also a good source of vitamin B1, vitamin B6, vitamin K, biotin, fiber, potassium, and thiamine.

Ingredients
1 cup organic raisins, soaked 1 hour, and finely chopped
2 cups carrot pulp, from juicing carrots
¼ cup maple syrup
1 ½ Tbsp. tahini
1/8 tsp. ground cloves
1/8 tsp. ground nutmeg
1 tsp. vanilla bean powder
1/8 tsp. ground cinnamon

½ cup unsweetened shredded coconut
2 cups walnuts, chopped finely

Yield: 6 Servings
Serving Size: About 1 slice

Place raisins, carrot pulp, maple syrup, and tahini in large bowl. Stir to mix. Add cloves, nutmeg, vanilla, cinnamon, and coconut. Stir again just until moist. Mix in the walnuts ½ cup at a time. Press the mixture firmly into small square pan or glass pie plate. Let set for at least 1 hour. Frost with Raw Cream 'Cheese' Frosting. Enjoy!

Raw Cashew Cookies

Cashew nuts are packed with energy, antioxidants, minerals and vitamins that are essential for robust health. They are also high in calories; 100 gm of cashews provide 553 calories. They are packed with soluble dietary fiber and numerous photochemical that help protect us from disease and cancer.

<u>Ingredients</u>
1/3 cup maple syrup
1/3 cup almond milk
¼ cup raw cacao powder
3 Tbsp. cashew butter
1 tsp. vanilla powder
1 ½ cups oats
¼ cup pecans, optional

Yield: 8 Servings
Serving Size: About 1 cookie

In a blender, combine maple syrup, almond milk, and cacao powder; blend until smooth. Add cashew butter and continue blending until cashew butter is dissolved. Transfer to a medium bowl, and add the vanilla, oats, and pecans. Stir well until all ingredients are mixed. Form into small cookies. Enjoy!

Raw Cream 'Cheese' Frosting

This frosting is so delicious and light you will never know it's healthy!

Ingredients
1 cup raw cashews
3 Tbsp. fresh lemon juice
¼ cup maple syrup
1 tsp. vanilla bean powder

Yield: 6 Servings
Serving: About 1/6 of small cake

Puree all ingredients in a food processor at high speed to create a smooth, creamy, consistency. Then pour or spread over cake. Enjoy!

Raw Oatmeal Fudge

Oatmeal contains insoluble fiber, which stays in the stomach longer and helps you feel full. The fiber in oats also has many health benefits. Carob powder is frequently used as a chocolate substitute in vegan recipes. Carob is rich in a number of nutrients and antioxidants and may help lower cholesterol levels.

<u>Ingredients</u>
1 cup rolled oats
¾ cup carob powder
¼ cup sunflower seeds, ground into a fine powder
½ cup raw almond nut butter
5 Medjool dates, pitted & soaked 3 hours
¼ cup maple syrup
¾ cup walnuts or pecans, chopped
¼ cup sesame seeds, ground

Yield: 16 Servings
Serving Size: About 1 square

Place first five ingredients in a food processor and blend well. With machine still running, add maple syrup until mixture forms a ball. Remove from food processor and fold in nuts. Press mixture into an 8 X 8 square pan lined with parchment paper or oiled. Chill one hour or overnight; cut into squares and serve. Keep covered in air tight container in refrigerator. Enjoy!

Blueberries and Cream Kale Chips

Blueberries and blueberry juice can alleviate urinary tract infections. Blueberries are a good source of vitamins, minerals, dietary fiber, and flavonoids. They are very low in fat and sodium. Blueberries contain 14 mg. of Vitamin C and 0.8 mg of Vitamin E per cup.

Ingredients
1 cup blueberries (fresh or frozen)
1 cup cashews, soaked and drained
1 cup distilled water
¾ cup agave nectar or sweetener of your choice
1 Tbsp. cinnamon
1 lemon juiced or 2-3 Tbsp.
2 tsp. pure vanilla extract
Celtic sea salt to taste
1 bunch kale, washed, trimmed and stem removed

Yield: 4 Servings
Serving Size: About 3/4 cup

Combine all ingredients (except kale) into a blender. Blend until smooth; add sea salt to taste. Massage kale with the blueberries mixture until coated. Place kale on an Excalibur ParrFlex sheet and dehydrate 8-10 hours or until desired consistency is reached. Store in an airtight container. Enjoy!!!

Note: You can also cook this in a conventional oven at the lowest setting, checking every 5 minutes. When chips appear dry, they are ready.

Carrot Pulp Bread

<u>Ingredients</u>
2 cups flax Seeds, ground
½ cup sesame seeds, ground
½ cup sunflower seeds, ground
4 cups carrot pulp
½ red bell pepper
1 red apple, chopped
½ cup raisins, soaked 15 min
1 ½ cups water
½ tsp. salt to taste

Yield: 12 Servings
Serving Size: About 2 sandwiches

In a food processor, combine carrot pulp, bell pepper, apple, raisins, and salt to taste. Mix well, then add water and mix again. Put flax seeds, sesame seeds, and sunflower seeds in a bowl, then add liquid mixture to seeds and mix well. Spread mixture on dehydrator tray and divide into

9 pieces. Dehydrate at 105 degrees for 8 hours; flip and dry for another 1-2 hours or until desired texture is reached. Bread should be dry but pliable. Bread will last up to two weeks in refrigerator. Enjoy!

Cheesy Kale Chips

   Nutritional yeast is an inactive yeast that is a favorite among vegans because of its unique nutty, cheesy flavor and similarity to cheese when added to food. It's also a reliable food source of B-12.

Ingredients
1 cup cashews, soaked 2 hours and drained
1 yellow bell pepper, seeded
3 Tbsp. fresh lemon juice
1 Tbsp. pure maple syrup
3 Tbsp. nutritional yeast
½ tsp. onion powder
½ tsp. turmeric
½ tsp. Celtic sea salt
1 large bunch kale, washed and stems removed

Yield: 4 Servings
Serving Size: About 3/4 cup

Combine all ingredients (except kale) in blender. Puree until smooth. Add sea salt. Massage kale with the cashew mixture until well coated. Place on Excalibur Parrflex sheet, and dehydrate for 8-10 hours or until desired crispness is reached. Enjoy!

Easy Super-Food Chia Pudding

Goji juice has become popular as a health drink. Goji berries are considered a superfood because of the large quantity of antioxidants and many health benefits they offer.

Ingredients
3 Tbsp. chia seeds
2 Tbsp. goji berries
1 inch cube ginger root, ground
1 cup non-dairy milk
2 Tbsp. maple syrup

Yield: 2 Servings
Serving Size: About 3/4 cup

Combine all ingredients in a small bowl. Stir for 15 minutes, mixing all ingredients well; let set in refrigerator for 30 to 60 minutes. Enjoy!!!

Note: Fresh fruit may also be added, before serving.

Home-Made Corn Chips

Make these corn chips in the late summer, when the corn is luscious and sweet. There is nothing like corn chips with "cheese."

Ingredients
3 ½ cups sweet corn, fresh or frozen
2 cloves garlic
1 tsp. chili powder
1 tsp. tomato powder, see tomato powder-dehydrator

Yield: 8 Servings
Serving Size: About 2-4 chips

Chop corn in a food processor with S blade until it's fine. Add garlic, chili powder, and tomato; process until combined. Spread onto a dehydrator tray about 1/8" thick. Score diagonally left to right, then across right to left into triangles (or preferred shape). Dehydrate about 5 hours or to desired texture. These are super. Enjoy!

Irresistible Ice Cream

Nothing is as refreshing as a bowl of ice cream on a summer night. But forget about the heavy cream you thought you needed to make scrumptious ice cream. This ice cream is made with homemade non-dairy milk and your favorite fruit.

<u>Ingredients</u>
6 cups almond milk
12 Medjool dates, pitted
½ cup raw honey
2 tsp. vanilla bean powder
¼ cup Udo's 3-6-9 Oil Blend

Yield: 8 Serving
Serving Size: About 3/4 cup

In blender, add all ingredients and blend until smooth. Freeze according to ice cream maker directions. This is a base for any ice cream you would like. You can add any sweet fruit, in the amount you prefer, also carob powder or mint herb. Enjoy!

Home-Made Tomato Powder

In the late summer time when all your tomatoes ripen at the same time or your local fruit market is almost giving away tomatoes; that is the time to make tomato powder. You can use tomato powder in soups, on top of fresh vegetable juice, in enchilada sauce, or really anywhere that calls for more of a "tomato" flavor.

Ingredients
6 lbs. tomatoes
Cooking spray

Yield: 4-6oz.
Serving Size: About 1-2 tsp.

Wash and core the tomatoes. There is no need to drain the tomatoes of their seeds or liquid. Slice tomatoes very thin (approximately 1/8"). Spray the screened
140

dehydrator cooking tray with nonstick cooking spray. Place sliced tomatoes on screened dehydrator trays; dehydrate at 145 degrees F for the first hour. After 1 hour, lower temperature to 105 degrees F; continue to dehydrate. After 5 hours, open dehydrator and flip tomatoes over. Continue to dehydrate until slices are completely dehydrated, dry, and crisp. Remove and place in high speed blender. Blend to a fine powder; store in an airtight jar or zip lock bag. Enjoy!

'Salmon' Pate

Almonds are rich in monounsaturated fatty acids that aid in lowering LDLs (bad cholesterol) in the human body. Almonds are also an excellent source of Vitamin E. They are gluten-free. Almonds are packed with B-complex groups of vitamins such as riboflavin, niacin, thiamin, vitamin B6, and folate; they also contain manganese, potassium, calcium, iron, magnesium, zinc, and selenium.

Ingredients
2 cups almonds, soaked overnight
1 cup celery, finely chopped
½ cup green onions, chopped
2 cups carrot pulp
3 tsp. lime juice
Dulse flakes
½ tsp. dried dill
½ tsp. Celtic sea salt

Parsley

Yield: 12 Servings
Serving Size: About ½ cup

Run the almonds through a
Champion juicer or blend until smooth.
Mix all ingredients (except parsley) in a
medium bowl, adding the Dulse flakes to
taste. Form the mixture into a rounded
loaf, and garnish with parsley. Enjoy!

Chia Seed Pudding with Coconut

Chia seeds are rich in omega-3 fatty acids and fiber. Because chia seeds expand when they get wet, they make you feel fuller longer. This makes them fantastic for weight loss.

Ingredients
2 ½ cups coconut milk, or non-dairy milk of your choice
½ cup raw cashew nuts, soaked 4 hours or overnight
1 Tbsp. vanilla extract
½ tsp. almond extract
½ cups medjool dates, pitted and chopped
½ cup maple syrup
1 tsp. powdered ginger
1 tsp. ground cinnamon
1/3 cup chia seeds
1/3 cup unsweetened coconut
1/3 cup walnuts, chopped, *optional*

Yield: 6 Servings
Serving Size: About 3/4 cup

Place coconut milk, cashews, vanilla extract, almond extract, and dates in a food processor, and blend until smooth. Pour the blended cashew mixture into a medium bowl. Add maple syrup, ginger, and cinnamon; stir until blended. Add chia seeds, coconut, and walnuts (if using), and stir. Wait a few minutes and stir again. You'll notice the chia seeds beginning to take on a gelatinous texture. Wait a few minutes, again, and stir. Wait and stir for a third time, then place pudding in the refrigerator for about one hour to overnight. Enjoy!

Raw Sweet Kale Soup

This kale soup can be made into a salad in the fall and winter months, but the hot steamy summer is made for this soup, chilled with light crackers or hearty bread

Ingredients
6 kale leaves, torn from stem and washed
¼ red apple, chopped
2 Tbsp. dried cranberries, soaked 15 min
2 Tbsp. shallots, chopped
½ orange, sliced
1 Tbsp. raw slivered almonds
1 Tbsp. garlic, minced
1 Tbsp. grapeseed oil
1 Tbsp. balsamic vinegar
1 Tbsp. olive oil
½ tsp. red chili flakes
½ tsp. oregano
1Tbsp raw organic honey
½ tsp. Celtic sea salt to taste
½ tsp. black pepper

Yield: 2 Servings
Serving Size: About 1 cup

Put kale in a food processor and pulse 7 times. Add apple, cranberries, and shallots. Pulse to mix twice; add orange and almonds, and mix again. Add the remaining ingredients and mix until desired consistency is reached. This soup tastes best cold. Enjoy!

148

Part Six

Salads

Part Six

Recipes in This Section

Black Beans, Corn, and Quinoa
Cucumber Tomato Salad
Creamy Spinach Salad
Tropical Fruit Salad
Black Bean Salsa
Rotini Salad Supreme
Singapore Slaw
Black-eyed peas 'Pickled'

Black Beans, Corn and Quinoa

Black beans, sometimes called turtle beans, are a good source of protein, fiber, iron, calcium, zinc, and vitamin B. A one cup serving of black beans provides nearly 15 grams of fiber. Eat black beans with quinoa, which is a super grain since it's a complete protein that's also rich in fiber and iron. Try Quinoa as an alternative to rice, potatoes, or pasta

Ingredients
6 cups cooked quinoa
1 (15 oz.) can black beans, rinsed and drained
1 (15 oz.) can non GMO corn, drained
4 medium fresh tomatoes, diced
½ cup red onion

½ cup cilantro, chopped
1 jalapeno pepper, seeded and diced
2 Tbsp. fresh lime juice
1 Tbsp. extra virgin olive oil
½ tsp. Celtic sea salt
¼ tsp. fresh ground black pepper
2 dashes of hot sauce, *optional*

Yield: 12 Servings
Serving Size: About 3/4 cup

Cook quinoa according to package directions (be sure to rinse it thoroughly first). In a medium bowl, combine black beans, corn, tomatoes, onions, cilantro, jalapeno, lime juice, oil, salt, black pepper, and hot sauce (if using). To serve, place a scoop of hot quinoa in a bowl or a plate and top with a generous scoop of the black bean mixture.
Stir before eating. Enjoy!

Cucumber Tomato Salad

This salad is so light, satisfying, and sweet that you will want to have it any time of day. Keep a bowl of it in the fridge to enjoy when you need a quick little pick-me-up.

Ingredients
4 medium 'chocolate' tomatoes
1 red onion, sliced thin
1 English cucumber, halved and sliced
2 Tbsp. balsamic vinegar
1 Tbsp. rice wine vinegar
1 tsp. raw honey
½ tsp. Celtic sea salt
¼ tsp. freshly ground black pepper
¼ cup fresh cilantro leaves, chopped

Yield: 1-2 Servings

Serving Size: 1 ½ cups

In a large bowl combine the tomatoes, onions, and cucumbers; set aside. In a small bowl, mix together the balsamic and rice wine vinegar, olive oil, honey, salt, and pepper. Drizzle the salad with the vinegar olive oil mixture and toss lightly to coat. Let the salad marinate in the refrigerator for one hour, then toss with cilantro and serve. Enjoy!

Creamy Spinach Salad

This salad is so easy to prepare and really delicious. Don't be surprised if you want to have it once a week! Refrigerate overnight for an unbelievable treat.

<u>Ingredients</u>
1 bunch spinach, washed
1 tsp. garlic powder
½ tsp. Celtic sea salt
1 lemon, juiced
2 Tbsp. extra virgin olive oil
½ red onion, sliced thin
2 Tbsp. Vegenaise

Yield: 1-2 Servings
Serving Size: About 1 ½ cup

In a small bowl mix together garlic powder, salt, lemon juice, olive oil, onion, and Vegenaise until blended. Set aside. Chop the spinach. Drizzle marinade over spinach and toss to coat. It helps to gently knead the spinach with your hands. Refrigerate at least 1 hour or overnight before serving. Enjoy!

Tropical Fruit Salad

This yummy fruit salad is a good dish to take on a picnic or enjoy as a summertime lunch. My family loves this salad with cornbread muffins.

<u>Ingredients</u>
1 medium pineapple, or 2 ½ cups, peeled and diced
1 large papaya, peeled, and diced
2 medjool dates, seeded and finely chopped
3 medium kiwi fruit, peeled and diced
2 mangoes, peeled and diced
1 large ripe banana, peeled sliced
1 Tbsp. fresh lime juice

Yield: 6 Servings
Serving Size: About 1 cup

In a large bowl, gently toss the fruit with the lime juice until all is well combined. Chill the salad for a few hours before serving. You can purchase a fresh pineapple already peeled and ready to be sliced or diced for about one dollar more. Enjoy!

Black Bean Salsa

I can never make enough of this spicy, colorful, sensational salsa when we entertain family and friends. This recipe is so easy to make; you can get the whole family involved!

Ingredients
1 can black beans, rinsed
1 small onion, diced
½ red bell pepper, diced
½ green bell pepper, diced
1 can organic corn
1 large tomato, diced
½ tsp. Celtic sea salt
2 Tbsp. fresh squeezed lime juice
2 tsp. cumin, or seasoning of choice
1 tsp. ground black pepper

Yield: 4 Servings
Serving Size: About ½ cup

Wash and prepare the fresh vegetables. Combine all ingredients in a medium mixing bowl. Use as a dip with tortilla or pita chips or serve in your favorite salad, sandwich, or wrap. Enjoy!

Rotini Salad Supreme

Cool and refreshing, this salad is fantastic to keep in the refrigerator for a quick snack.

Ingredients
4 oz. rotini pasta
1 carrot, shredded
½ cup red cabbage, shredded
½ red bell pepper, cut into thin strips
¼ cup celery, sliced thin
¼ cup dried cranberries, craisins
1 ½ Tbsp. yellow onion, minced
½ cup Vegenaise
½ tsp. Celtic sea salt
¼ tsp. freshly ground black pepper

Yield: 4 Servings
Serving Size: About ½ cup

Cook the rotini according to package directions. After cooking, run under cold running water to stop the pasta from continuing to cook. Drain the pasta and transfer to a large bowl. Add the carrots, red cabbage, bell pepper, celery, cranberries, and onion; set aside. In a small bowl mix Vegenaise, salt, and pepper; add to rotini mixture. Stir to combine. Refrigerate 30 minutes before serving. Enjoy!

Singapore Slaw

Cabbage is rich in various phytonutrients and vitamins A, C and K. Jicama is a low calorie root vegetable rich in vitamin C, which also provides healthy amounts of minerals like magnesium, copper, and iron.

<u>Ingredients</u>
3 cups shredded cabbage

1 carrot, julienne
1 ½ cups jicama, cut into strips
1 orange, peeled and sectioned
¼ red bell pepper, julienne
¼ yellow bell pepper, julienne
1 small red onion, thinly sliced
2 Tbsp. fresh cilantro, chopped
2 Tbsp. extra virgin olive oil
4 tsp. rice vinegar
1 Tbsp. raw organic agave nectar
1 tsp. sesame seeds, toasted

1 tsp. sesame seed oil
1 tsp. organic nama shoyu (unpasteurized soy sauce)
¼ tsp. dry mustard
¼ cup sliced almonds

Yield: 8 Servings
Serving Size: About 3/4 cup

In a large mixing bowl, combine cabbage, jicama, orange sections, bell peppers, red onion, and cilantro. Cover and chill 2-3 hours.
For dressing: combine olive oil, rice vinegar, agave nectar, sesame seeds, sesame oil, soy sauce, and dry mustard in a mason jar with a lid. Shake well and pour over salad. Toss lightly to coat. Sprinkle with sliced almonds. Enjoy

Black-eyed Peas 'Pickled'

<u>Ingredients</u>
2 cans (15-oz. each) black-eyed peas, drained
¼ yellow bell pepper, minced
¼ red bell pepper, minced
¼ green bell pepper, minced
¼ orange bell pepper, minced
1 small onion, minced
2 garlic cloves, minced
2 Tbsp. red wine vinegar
1/3 cup extra virgin olive oil
2 Tbsp. fresh thyme

Yield: 8 Servings

Serving Size: About ¾ cup

Pour the drained black-eyed peas into a medium airtight bowl; add the bell pepper, onion, and garlic. In another bowl combine the vinegar, olive oil, and thyme to form the marinade. Pour the marinade over the black-eyed pea mixture; cover and refrigerate overnight so that the flavors blend, stirring occasionally. Can be eaten cold, warm, or as a condiment. Enjoy!

Celebrity Vegans and Vegetarians

As you will see after reading through this list of celebrity Vegans/Vegetarians, you are in *good* company. Continue reading to see how many you recognize. This list is nowhere near complete; it is only a small sample.

1. Lea Michele- Animal rights Activist and vegan.

2. Bill Clinton- The former president dropped 30 pounds after cutting out meat and dairy in 2010.

3. Ellen DeGeneres- She has been a vegan for years and even had a vegan wedding

4. Alicia Silverstone- Silverstone has been a vegan since shortly after her "Clueless" days.

5. Carrie Underwood- PETA's sexiest vegetarian celebrity of 2005 and 2007. Carrie Underwood says she became a vegetarian at age 13 when she realized what happened to animals on her family farm.

6. Mike Tyson- The boxing champion has some serious muscle, and it's all plant-based.

7. Betty White- The 90-year-old actress is an animal activist and has been a vegan for years.

8. Denzel Washington- Denzel is a recent vegetarian, although he admits to cheating with chicken on occasion. But it's a start!

9. Andre 3000- After the release of *Outkast's* first album, Andre 3000 became a vegetarian. He has been meat-free since he was 22 years old.

10. Ben Stiller- The perpetual funny man gave up coffee and became a vegan in 2012.

11. Christian Bale - The *"Batman"* star gave up meat when he was just 9 years old, after reading "Charlotte's Web".

12. Kal Penn- Despite being famous for his ridiculous journey to White Castle, he is a strict vegetarian.

13. NeYo- NeYo made the decision to become vegan as part of a New Year's resolution. Later in life, he learned more about the various reasons to become a vegan and now adheres much more meaning to it.

14. Questlove- Roots drummer Questlove embraced a plant-based diet due to health reasons. He said he wanted to be the first member of the Hip-Hop generation to live past 60.

15. Richard Gere- The actor has been meat-free for over 30 years.

16. Sarah Silverman- Not only is Sarah a vegetarian; she is an activist for circus animals.

17. Steve O- He credits his vegetarianism to watching a Youtube video. At first, he said he was motivated by "Fern of Spiritual Consequences," but soon found that it simply made him feel good about himself.

18. Milo Ventimiglia- Named by PETA as 2009's sexiest Vegetarian, he has been a vegetarian since he was in the womb.

19. Oliver Wild- Wild was crowned 2010s sexiest Vegetarian by PETA.

20. Kellie Pickler- Kellie told "People Magazine" she stopped eating meat to improve her health, but changed her reasoning after discovering animal cruelty videos online.

21. Alec Baldwin- According to zimblo.com, Alec Baldwin choose an animal-free diet for the animals, for the environment, and for his health.

22. Christina Applegate- Actress and animal activist, Christina Applegate told PETA she stopped eating meat when she saw blood on her plate while at a restaurant.

23. Anna Paquin- The actress and the mother of twins may be surrounded by a lot of blood on the "True Blood" set; but in reality, she is a vegetarian.

24. Bruce Springsteen- Springsteen looks amazing at 63, and it may have something to do with his vegetarian diet.

25. Emily Deschanel- Zooey Deschanel's sister has been a vegan for 20 years. She explains, "Saying no to meat makes me feel stronger inside."

26. Peter Dinklage- The "Game of Thrones" star is a vegetarian, telling PETA, "I won't hurt a cat or a dog or a chicken or a cow. And I won't ask someone else to hurt them for me. That's why I am a vegetarian."

index

D

H

Tropical Fruit Salad, 157

L

Lemon Juice
 Blueberries and Cream Kale Chips, 128
 Cauliflower, Macaroni and
  'Cheese' 93
 'Cheesy' Kale chips, 132
 Classic Butternut Squash Humus, 74
 Green Olive Humus, 79
 Kale and Collard Energy Smoothie, 51
 Mama Suebee Ginger Banana
  Shake, 63
 Roasted red Pepper Humus, 70
 Spinach Creamy Salad, 84
 Super-Food Green Smoothie, 55
 White Beans and Roasted eggplant
  Humus, 81

M

Maca Powder
 Feel Good Smoothie, 65
 Super-Food Smoothie, 55